Keeping Fit

By Paul Bennett

🌱 Belitha Press

First published in Great Britain in 1997 by
Belitha Press Limited
London House, Great Eastern Wharf
Parkgate Road, London SW11 4NQ

Copyright in this format © Belitha Press Limited 1997
Text copyright © Paul Bennett

Editor: Veronica Ross
Series designer: Hayley Cove
Photographer: Claire Paxton
Illustrator: Cilla Eurich
Picture researcher: Diana Morris
Consultant: Elizabeth Atkinson

ISBN 1 85661 589 4

Printed in Hong Kong

Photo credits
Bubbles Photo Library: 16. Sally and Michael Greenhill: 21, 26. Zefa-Stockmarket: 17 Michael Heron, 26 Jost L. Pelaez.

Thanks to models Topel, Jodie, Ricky, Bianca, Meera, Stephen, Fiona.

Words in **bold** are explained in the list of useful words on pages 30 and 31.

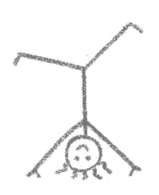

Contents

Your body   4
Keeping fit   6
Exercise is fun!   8
What makes me move?   10
Bones hold up your body   12
What are joints?   14
Broken bones   16
Skin deep   18
Cuts and grazes   20
Too much sun   22
Feeling ill   24
Protecting against disease   26
Keeping clean   28
Useful words   30
Index   32

Your body

What is the colour of
your skin, eyes and hair?
Is your hair long or
short, straight or curly?
What shape are you?
Are you tall or short?

We are all
different.
No one looks
exactly like
you. This
makes you
special.

Keeping fit helps your
body to stay **healthy**.
You also need
plenty of rest,
and to eat three
meals a day.

Your body is made up of millions of tiny **cells**. They make up your **bones**, skin, **blood** and all the other parts of your body.

You will use your body all your life, so it is important to look after yourself.

It's important to get plenty of sleep, so that you have lots of energy in the morning.

Keeping fit

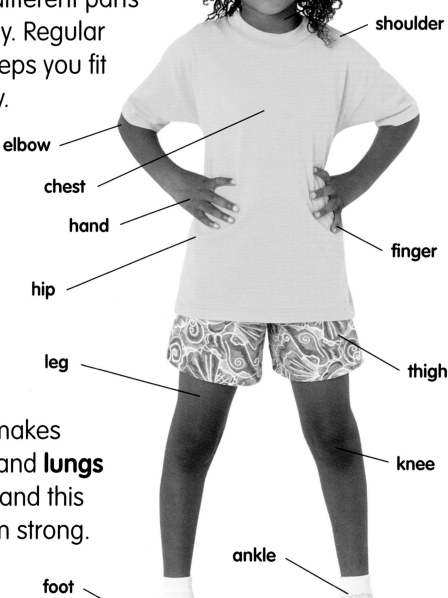

When you **exercise**, you use many different parts of your body. Regular exercise keeps you fit and healthy.

head

neck

shoulder

elbow

chest

hand

finger

hip

leg

thigh

knee

Exercising makes your **heart** and **lungs** work hard, and this makes them strong.

ankle

foot

toe

If you are fit and healthy, you will have lots of energy for running and playing.

Which parts of your body do you use when you run? Do you use the same parts when you swim?

Swimming is a great way to exercise. It uses most of the **muscles** in your body.

Exercise is fun!

Your body works better when it is used a lot. Think of the things you like to do. Running, playing football, skipping, cycling and roller skating all help to keep you fit.

Your body may become stiff if you do not use it.

Bending and stretching are other ways of exercising your body.

When you exercise, you breathe quickly. If you have been exercising hard, it may take a few minutes to get your breath back.

9

What makes me move?

Muscles make you move. You use your muscles when you play games, run, swim, breathe, smile and talk. Your heart is a muscle, too. It beats without you thinking about it.

When you bend your leg, you can feel the muscles working.

Many muscles work in pairs. As you bend your arm, the biceps muscle pulls your arm up. The triceps muscle pulls in the other direction and straightens out your arm. Muscles are attached to your bones by bands called tendons.

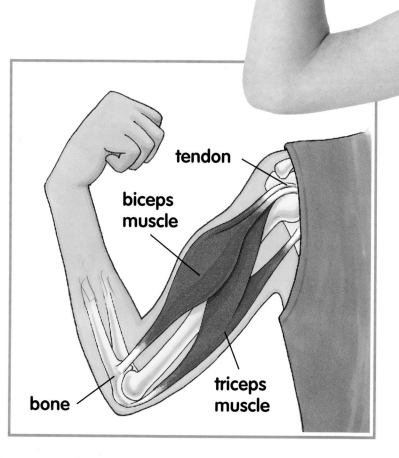

tendon

biceps muscle

bone

triceps muscle

Bones hold up your body

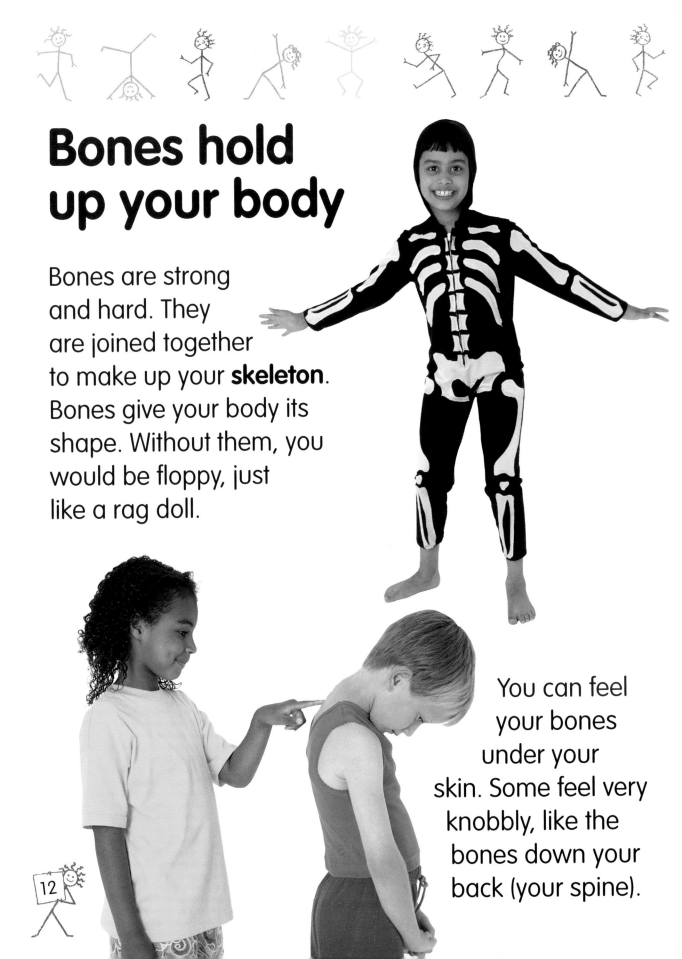

Bones are strong and hard. They are joined together to make up your **skeleton**. Bones give your body its shape. Without them, you would be floppy, just like a rag doll.

You can feel your bones under your skin. Some feel very knobbly, like the bones down your back (your spine).

12

You have 27 bones in each hand. The bones in your fingers feel smooth and straight.

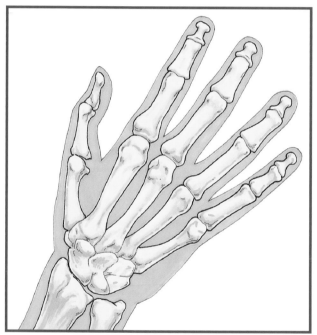

Bones protect the soft parts inside your body from injury. Your **skull** protects your brain and your **ribs** protect your heart and lungs.

13

What are joints?

Bones are hard and do not bend. Your body can only bend at the joints. These are the places where two bones meet.

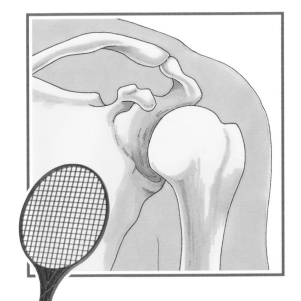

Your arm is attached to your shoulder by a **ball and socket joint**.

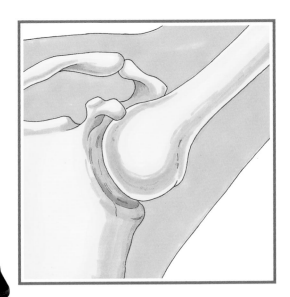

A ball and socket joint allows you to move your arm in almost any direction.

Try swinging your arms round and round and up and down.

Your hips have ball and socket joints, too

Your elbows and knees are **hinge joints**. They can only move backwards and forwards, like a door hinge.

You also have hinge joints in your fingers.

15

Broken bones

Bones grow and change shape just like the rest of you. And when they break, they mend themselves.

A break in a bone is called a fracture. A **plaster cast** keeps the broken pieces of bone firmly together.

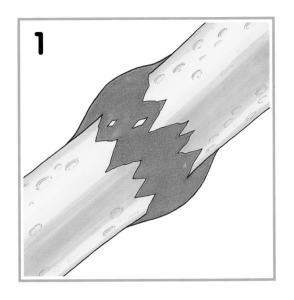

1 When a bone breaks, blood around the break hardens and covers the broken ends.

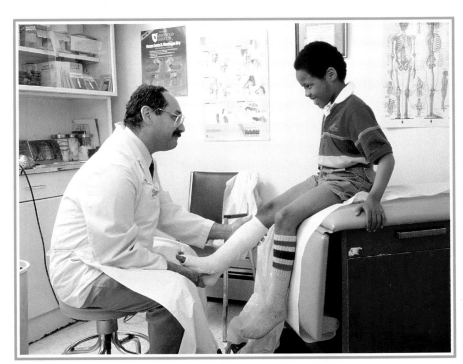

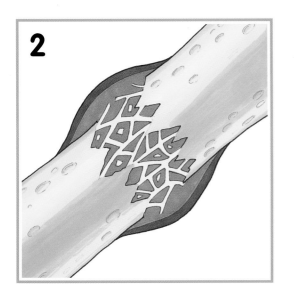

2

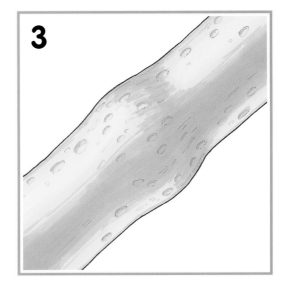

3

2 New bone grows on each side of the break, and joins the broken bones together.

3 After about 12 weeks, the break has **healed**, and the plaster cast can be taken off.

Bones are hard and strong, but they may break if you fall or have an accident.

17

Skin deep

Skin is waterproof and very tough. It keeps harmful things, such as dust and **germs**, out of your body.

Your skin is soft, but stretchy. It allows you to move about.

Your skin never wears out! Old skin cells are replaced by new ones all the time.

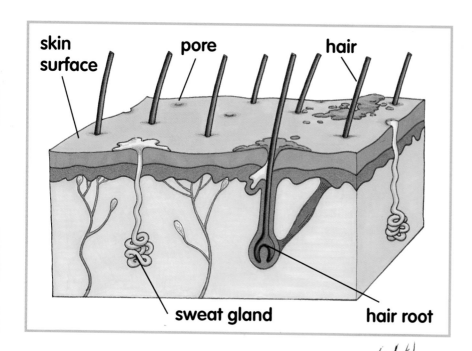

skin surface

pore

hair

sweat gland

hair root

This is a drawing of the surface of your skin. When you are cold, the hairs stand up straight.

Skin keeps you cool. When you run, your body becomes hot, and **sweat** oozes out of your skin through tiny holes called pores.

As the sweat trickles over your skin, your body cools down.

Cuts and grazes

If you **graze** or cut yourself, blood trickles out of your skin. Soon the blood stops and dries to form a hard **scab**. The scab covers the wound and stops germs getting into your body.

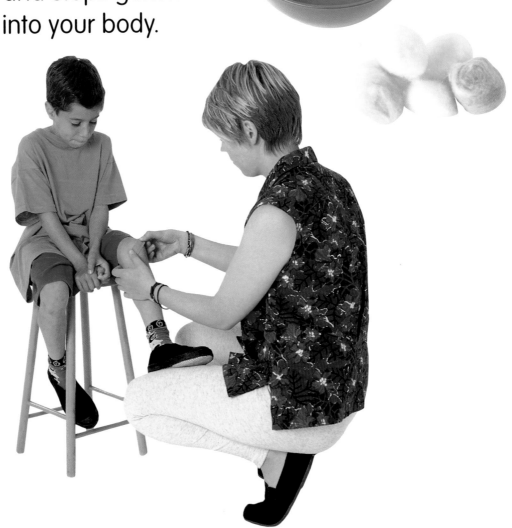

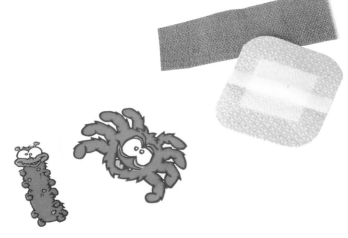

Wash the wound with water to clean it. A **bandage** or **plaster** helps to keep out the germs.

A scab forms to protect the broken skin.

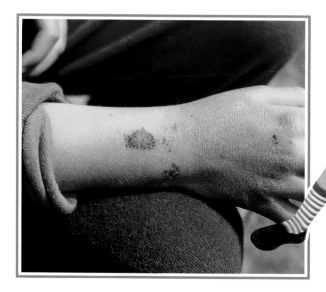

New skin cells grow under the scab, and the wound starts to heal.

Don't pick at the scab! It will fall off when the skin is completely healed.

Too much sun

Playing out in the sun is fun.
It makes you feel good.
But too much
sun can be
harmful.

If you are badly
sunburnt, your skin
turns red and sore.

Painful bubbles
of fluid, called
blisters, may form
on the burnt skin.

22

Doctors believe that too much sunlight causes a dangerous **disease** called skin cancer. This can be treated, but it is best to avoid too much sun.

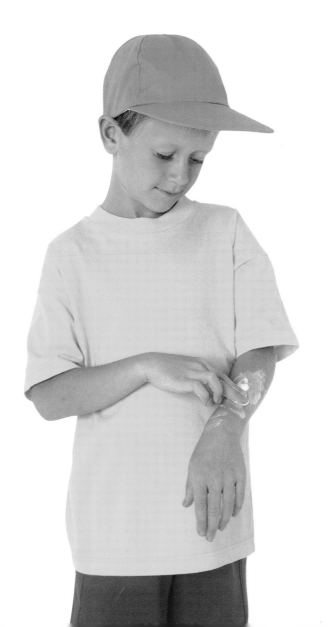

Cover Up!
Wear a hat and T-shirt. Use a special cream to protect your skin. Stay in the shade when the sun is at its strongest during the middle of the day.

Feeling ill

Have you ever had a cough or cold? It is best to stay in bed when you are feeling ill.

If your illness does not go away, you should see a doctor. He or she will decide what treatment will make you better.

You may have to go to a hospital if your illness is serious. The doctors and nurses will look after you. If you need to stay in hospital, your mum or dad, or a grown-up friend, can usually stay with you.

Protecting against disease

Is it true that coughs and sneezes spread diseases? Yes!

When you sneeze, air shoots out of your mouth and nose at about 160 km per hour – the speed of a hurricane. So do not cough or sneeze over other people!

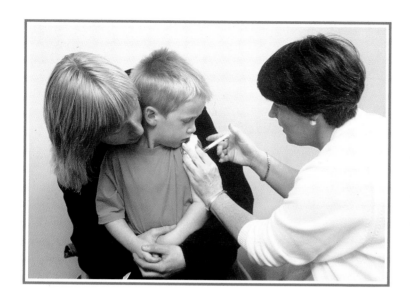

Doctors protect you against serious diseases by giving you an **injection** or some medicine to swallow.

Chickenpox and mumps are two diseases that most people get when they are young. Once you have had them, you are unlikely to get them again.

Keeping clean

Keeping clean keeps your body healthy. It's important to wash every day, and to keep your hair clean.

Germs are all around you, even though you can't see them. Always wash your hands before eating, and after you have been to the toilet.

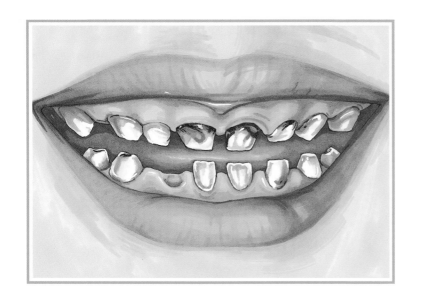

If you do not brush your teeth regularly your teeth may **decay**.

Every day your skin **sheds** millions of dead cells, and produces **oils** and sweat. If these stay on your skin for long, your body begins to smell nasty.

Useful words

Ball and socket joint
A joint that can move in many different directions.

Bandage
A special covering for a wound.

Blood
The red liquid that is pumped around your body by your heart.

Bones
The strong and hard parts of your body.

Cells
Tiny parts that make up your body.

Decay
To go bad or to rot.

Disease
Illness or sickness.

Exercise
Using your body by running, swimming, cycling, and so on.

Germs
Living things that are too small to be seen with the naked eye. They can make you ill.

Graze
To scrape your skin against something hard.

Healed
Made healthy again.

Healthy
Strong and well.

Heart
The muscle that pumps blood around your body.

Hinge joints
Joints that move backwards and forwards.

Injection
A way of protecting you against illness.

Lungs
The spongy areas in your chest that you use when breathing.

Muscles
The soft, stretchy parts of your body that make you move.

Oils
Greasy liquids from the skin.

Plaster
A small covering for a cut or graze.

Plaster cast
A strong covering for a broken bone.

Ribs
The bones in your chest.

Scab
The hard crust that forms over a cut or graze.

Shed
To throw off.

Skeleton
The bones in your body.

Skull
The bony part of your head.

Sunburnt
To have burnt skin after being in the hot sun.

Sweat
Wetness from the skin.

Index

ball and socket
    joint 14
bandage 21
biceps muscle 11
blisters 22
blood 5, 16, 20
bones 5, 12-13, 14,
    16-17
brain 13

cells 5, 18, 21, 29
chickenpox 27
coughing 26
cuts 20-21

diseases 26-27

elbows 15
exercise 6-7, 8-9

fingers 13, 15
fracture 16

germs 18, 20, 21,
    28

graze 20

hair 4, 19
heart 6, 10, 13
hinge joints 15
hips 15
hospital 25

illness 24-25
injection 27

joints 14-15

knees 15

lungs 6, 13

medicine 27
mumps 27
muscles 7, 10-11

oils 29

plaster 21
plaster cast 16
pores 19

ribs 13

scabs 20, 21
skeleton 12
skin 4, 18-19, 20,
    21, 22, 23, 29
skin cancer 23
skull 13
sleep 5
sneezing 26
spine 12
sun 22-23
sunburn 22
sweat 19, 29
swimming 7

teeth 29
tendons 11
tooth decay 29
triceps muscle 11

washing 28